Making Music with the Young Child with Special Needs

Child with Special Needs

A Guide for Parents

books of related interest

Music Therapy in Health and Education
Edited by Margaret Heal and Tony Wigram
ISBN1 85302 175 X

Children with Special Needs 2nd edition
Assessment, Law and Practice – Caught in the Act
Harry Chasty and John Friel
ISBN 1 85302 155 5

Movement Activities for Children with Learning Difficulties
Bren Pointer
ISBN 1 85302 167 9

Making Music with the Young Child with Special Needs

A Guide for Parents

Elaine Streeter

Jessica Kingsley Publishers
London and Bristol, Pennsylvania

94-91

First published and distributed in the United Kingdom by
    Music Therapy Publications (ISBN 0-9507145 0 X)

New edition published in 1993 by
    Jessica Kingsley Publishers Ltd
    116 Pentonville Road
    London N1 9JB

    Copyright © 1993 Elaine Streeter
    Photographs by Prue Bramwell-Davis
    Cover photo copyright????????

British Library Cataloguing in Publication Data
    Streeter, Elaine
    Making Music with the Young Child with
    Special Needs: Guide for Parents
    I. Title
    784.19
    ISBN 1-85302-187-3

Printed and Bound in Great Britain by
Biddles Ltd., Guildford and Kings Lynn

Contents

Acknowledgements

Thanks to:
Jemima, Claire, David, Kelly, Emma, and Paddy.
All the staff at the Children's Day Nursery and at the
Child Development Centre, Charing Cross Hospital.
The parents for their co-operation.

With special thanks to the late Dr Hugh Jolly who
supported and encouraged my work with young children
at the Child Development Centre, Charing Cross Hospital

A note on language

'She' has been used throughout this book, but 'she' embraces 'he'.

Introduction

Young children enjoy music and find it exciting. This is true for all children even if they are have physical or learning disabilities or if they are deaf or language disordered. A lot of parents would like to know how they can use this interest in music to help their child to develop. This booklet is designed to help you make the most of your child's interest in music, as early as possible, by discussing the ways in which music can be used and showing you how to start playing simple musical instruments at home.

Part 1

How Can Music Help?

How Can Music Help?

Making music can help your child in a number of ways.

Language Development

Whether or not your child can speak, music can help to give her some of the listening experiences she needs to develop language. Because she is interested in the sound of music your child will automatically be listening more carefully and this is one of the first steps towards using language. Children understand a lot more language than they can use at first; they have been listening to all the talking going on around them for a long time. Then they begin to use speech themselves. The child with special needs may have difficulty in concentration and this will affect her listening ability. Although her hearing may be quite normal, she may not be making much sense of what she hears. By playing simple musical games together you will be helping to focus your child's listening ability and at the same time giving her the experience of 'Conversation'. You won't be using words, you will be using a language she already understands – music. Having musical conversations can help your child to understand what real language is all about; she may not understand why one person stops talking and someone else starts; she may not realise that they are listening to one another. So, sharing a musical phrase and answering a musical phrase are two very simple conversational games that can help.

The more the child enjoys music, the more likely she is to make vocal sounds herself. If the child is at a pre-speech level, music can encourage her to explore and imitate sounds. When the child begins to use words, music can help to emphasise the meaning, intonation and rhythm of language.

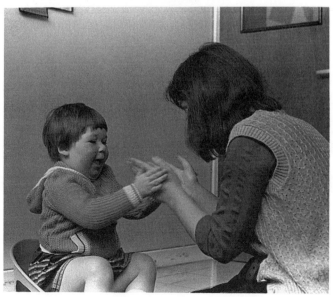

Play

As you probably know, play is going to be very important for your child. However, it may be difficult for her to start playing if she does not understand how to use objects. Playing music can help the child understand that using objects can make something happen. If the child can enjoy making music with simple instruments, she may be able to learn more quickly that holding on to something can lead to using it. Because music is an immediate experience, very little time is lost between holding and doing, so you may be able to sustain her attention long enough for her to learn that it is worth holding on to things. Later on, when playing is easier, music can help the child to explore imaginatively. Children love to listen to stories with music; their imagination is stimulated by the different musical ideas in nursery rhymes, for example, and this can help them eventually to develop imaginary games with cars, dolls and animals.

Physical Development

For children with physical disabilities, musical activity can help to define movement sequences. Because the rhythm in music invites movement, your child is likely to be interested in trying to move with the music. You can make the most of this motivation by creating a musical game of crawling, walking or even stretching out. Musical rhythm is not merely a diversion. It will actually help your child to coordinate muscle patterns. Coordination of movement is essential for crawling, walking and running, so even if your child is not ready for any of these movements, giving her the opportunity to play rhythmic music is going to give her the chance to attempt physical coordination. Wanting to move accurately can help the child achieve better coordination and music makes children want to move.

Relationships

Some children with special needs find it difficult to relate to people. Others have difficult personalities and develop anti-social behaviour. It can be hard for parents to find a way of communicating with a child who gives them so little to go on. Music is not the complete answer but it can provide a time of togetherness when your child can be a little easier to get on with because of her interest in music. Anybody who has ever played music with other people, sung in a choir or played in a band will know that a communal musical experience can be very intimate, even if you don't know the other people. Music really does bring people together. There is no reason why this should not be the case between parents and children, especially if other forms of communication are difficult. Music can make your child feel less isolated and more 'normal'. Sharing music together can also give you the opportunity to praise her achievements which in turn will make her want to try harder, not just to play music but to attract your attention generally.

Part 2

How to Get Started

How Do I Begin?

By now you are probably saying to yourself, 'Yes, this sounds a good idea, but I'm not musical enough, I can't sing, I can't play an instrument and I certainly can't read music!'

First of all, none of the following suggestions will require you to learn a complicated instrument or to read music, and, most important of all, everybody is musical. You may have been told in the past that you sing out of tune or that you can't keep time. This is true for a very very small minority of people. However, if you start to think of musical enjoyment rather than performance, you will start to relax about the idea of playing music. Begin by thinking about your favourite song, record or piece of music. If you can sing it to yourself or dance to it or tap your foot to it, it means you are musical. The first step in making music with your child is to understand that YOU are MUSICAL.

Here are some suggestions to help you feel more confident about singing and playing:

1. Try quietly humming to yourself.

2. If you listen to the radio, try singing along to the music when nobody is around.

3. Sing to yourself at some time during the day, for a week; you will be surprised how quickly your voice improves as you get used to using it.

4. Try moving in time to your favourite dance record and then clapping in time to your movements.

5. If you like classical music, listen to choral pieces such as Bach's *St. Mathew Passion*. Join in the easy parts with some 'La La's'.

6. Listen to the same pieces or songs regularly. Get to know them and join in.

Helping your child through music making could be a long-term project so there is no point in rushing into it. Take as much time as you need to build up your confidence. You may want to make time to listen to some live music, go to a concert or get together with someone else who would like to use music with their child.

94-91

What Do I Need to Get?

You won't need to buy a lot of new things at once, but you should aim towards building up a small collection of well-made instruments. It is better to be limited to a skin-head tambour than to have a lot of plastic drums and whistles which are cheap but sound horrible. The sound of the instruments is very important; the clearer the sound, the more it will help the child to focus her listening. Well-made instruments are expensive; however, they do last for a long time. It is worth checking with your GP to see whether you can get them supplied through the hospital Occupational Therapy department. If they can be described as 'aids' you may be able to get one or two things through the National Health Service. Alternatively, your local portage worker, toy library or opportunity play group may be able to help.

The following list of instruments covers all the activities described in this booklet. Look through the activities and decide which of them is relevant to your child's developmental level. There is obviously no point in getting a xylophone, for instance if the child cannot hold and use an object, so think about the child's level of skill rather than the instrument when choosing what to buy first.

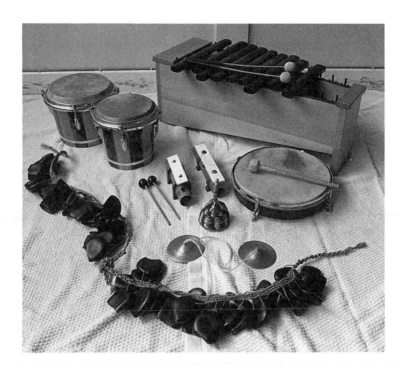

Basic instruments to collect

Skin tambour

Skin tambourine (covered with a head, not an open ring)

Chime bar C above middle C

Chime bar F below middle C (different colour from Chime bar C)

Felt beaters. two pairs, preferably with cork handles

Chime bar beaters, hard. Two pairs

African bean rattles, two different sounds

Reed horns, two (These come with a set of different pitch pipes included)

Wooden bongo drums

Wooden xylophone (not metal)

I would suggest you start by buying a tambour, a chime bar and some beaters.

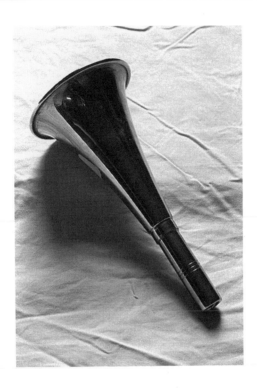

Most shops stock a wide range of educational instruments and will send a catalogue.

Rattles, cymbals and free-standing drums can sometimes be purchased more cheaply from ethnic shops or craft shops.

For further help with local suppliers contact:

The National Music and Disability
    Information Service,
Dartington Hall
Totnes
Devon. TQ9 6EJ
Tel: 0803 866701.

Planning Some Music Time

You probably know from experience that having a routine is important for the day-to-day care of your child. It is also important to define your music time as clearly as possible so that the child can anticipate making music. The following suggestions are to help you plan a music time lasting about 15 minutes at first.

1. Make music when your child is alert, at the same time of the day, in the same room.

2. Make music in a place where you are not going to be disturbed by other children or the noise of television or radio. Remember, you are trying to sharpen your child's listening, so she will need as much silence around her music as possible.

3. Only use the instruments for your music time. Don't let the child play aimlessly with them or they will soon lose their interest.

4. Because you will be listening carefully to what the child is doing, it is important to keep music-making a one-to-one activity to begin with. Later on, when the child is ready to share and take turns, you can

involve other children, but always be sure that the child with special needs is setting the pace. Only involve other children if it is adding to the activity rather than detracting from it.

5. Plan which instruments you are going to use BEFORE you start and have a clear idea of what you are aiming at.

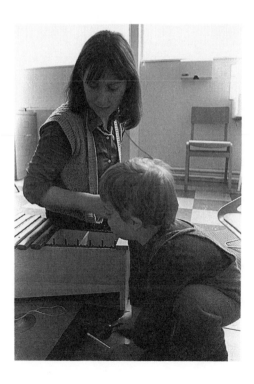

How to Play

There is a whole variety of ways you can use the simple percussion instruments listed. The following activities are merely guide-lines for your own playing. In the photographs you can see how different children have played the instruments and how we have developed games together. You may want to use the games as starting points for your playing. They are suggestions and may not work in exactly the same way as they did for the children in the illustrations. You must develop a flexible approach to the instruments and adapt the following activities to suit the needs of your child.

Before you start, there are a few questions you should keep in mind as you go along:

- Is the child able to 'keep up' with you, or is the music too fast or too slow?

- Is the child listening to what she is doing, or is she just banging away on the drum?

- Can the child hear both you and herself?

- Is the child repeating the same pattern over and over again, and losing herself in the activity?

- Is there enough space for 'questions' and 'answers' in the music?

- Is the child using the instrument meaningfully, or has she reverted to sucking or chewing?

During music time you can afford to have high standards. After all, it is only 15 minutes or so, and 15 minutes concentrated effort from the child is worth guiding carefully.

Part 3

Activities

The activities are labelled as very easy, easy, and more difficult. You don't have to work through them from 1 to 13. At first, choose ones you think the child can achieve, and then later move on to more difficult ones.

ACTIVITY ONE

Exploring the Drum

It is a good idea to sit opposite the child, on the floor.

First, present the drum to her, so that the flat surface faces her.

Hold the drum whilst she explores it.

Wait and see what she does.

Show her that she can produce a sound by tapping it, once.

DON'T tap out a complicated pattern in the hope that she will imitate it. You must take your cues from her rather than lead the playing, so keep holding the drum and direct her hands towards it.

Wait and see what she does.

When she makes a strong tap, praise her in your usual way.

Hold her hand and let it drop onto the drum. As it hits the drum make a sound yourself to accentuate what the child has done, say 'Bang!' or 'Crash'.

Work towards repetition; if you find something attracts her attention – repeat it.

Be as free as you can with your own vocal sounds as she plays.

Let her show you what speed she wants to play at.

DON'T beat with her hands on the drum – she may need more time to explore single sounds before she will be able to play 'in time'.

Activity Two

Up and Down Tambourine Game

This is a very simple sound conversation. The aim is to encourage imitation and create a dialogue.

Sitting opposite the child, get her attention.

Raise your hand to eye level whilst saying, 'UP'.

Hold your hand in the 'up' position for a moment.

As you say, 'DOWN' bring your hand down onto the tambourine.

Repeat 'UP' and 'DOWN'.

Present the drum to the child.

Get her attention and say 'UP' – wait for her to start raising her arm.

If she needs help do the action with her.

Hold the arm 'UP' for a second and then say 'DOWN' as she brings it down.

Try to make your voice go up and down as you play.

Repeat the sequence so that you are playing alternately.

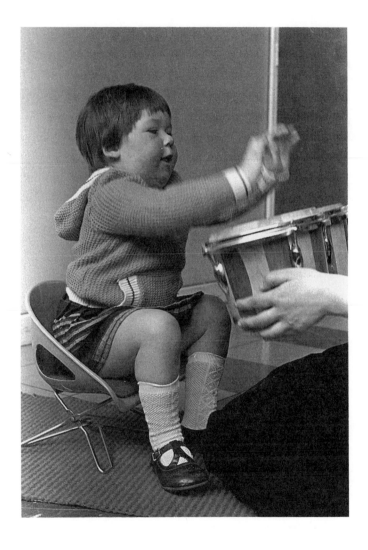

ACTIVITY THREE

Holding and Using a Beater

At first it may be difficult to interest the child in using the beaters. However when she realises that she can make a better sound on the tambour, she will start to use it more readily. For those children who throw objects, learning to hold and use, rather than hold and throw, can be an important step forward, so it is worth persevering. Use an activity which the child has already enjoyed or a song she knows to entice her into holding a beater.

Position yourself with two beaters at the ready.

Offer the child a beater and let her explore it in her usual way.

After a short exploration begin your favourite beating game or song.

Try to avoid the beater being thrown or dropped because once this has happened it can appear more interesting to throw it than use it.

If necessary hold your hand firmly around the child's to support her grip.

Be careful to follow her speed of beating.

Do not expect the child to enjoy using the beater the first time. If she is very resistive it may be enough simply to have the experience of making one tap.

DON'T lose patience and beat the drum for her; it is very important to listen to what the child is trying to do, however primitive it may be. What you are aiming at is supporting and encouraging the child's attempts at playing rather than imposing musical patterns upon her. The child will very soon lose interest if she feels she cannot keep up.

ACTIVITY FOUR

Using Bongo Drums

Bongos are useful as standing drums. Put them on the floor and they are a sturdy instrument with a good sound; hold them and they are light enough to be moved quickly towards the child.

Later on, bongos are useful for getting the child to make alternate hand movements. This in turn will make her more aware of her two hands. In the case of cerebral-palsied children, or those with immature physical development, you can concentrate on getting the hands forward and down onto the drums simultaneously as this will help to increase balance and symmetrical muscle patterns.

Hold the drums so that the child does not have to reach down very far, at about chin level with the child. Tilt them towards her so that she can see what she is doing.

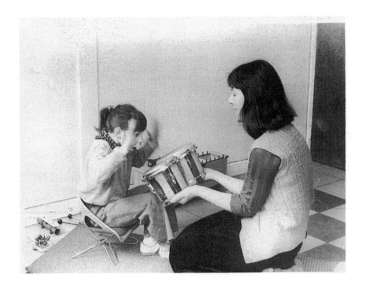

Let the child set the pace of the beating and sing to her as she beats.

Sing –   'Annie's beating on the BONG-GOS'
         'Annie's beating on the BONG-GOS'
         (*Or David's beating or Susie's beating –
         according to the child's name*).

ACTIVITY FIVE

Singing Songs to the Child's Drumming

When the child is able to sustain tapping at a regular pace, try extending the child's activity by singing to her as she plays. At first this may seem impossible, but once you have tried it you will find it is really not that difficult and will give the child a lot of stimulation. Get to know some simple tunes, possibly nursery rhymes or anything that you enjoy and can remember. Substitute new words for the words of the song. For example, instead of *Twinkle Twinkle, Little Star* sing – 'Dan is beating on the drum.' Make up your own words to describe what the child is doing. Choose two or three nursery rhymes to get to know because, however soppy they may seem, children love them. *BaBa Black Sheep, Humpty Dumpty,* and *Jack and Jill* are quite adequate. If you cannot remember how they go, get hold of a cassette recording or a record and learn them. However, at this early stage DON'T use the record as a substitute for your own singing. The singing needs to be flexible, following the speed of the child's playing instead of dictating her speed.

Getting to Know a Song

Choose one song to get to know, either your own or a nursery rhyme.

Sing in time to the child's tapping.

When she knows the end of the song, try delaying the last line slightly so that she has to listen to the words in order to know when to stop. This way, the child will have to listen to the sounds of the words and the length of the phrase.

Accenting the Phrase

Sing the song whilst holding the drum out of reach.

Bring the drum towards her as you finish the end of the line. Only let her tap on the last beat.

e.g.   'Jack and Jill went up the... hill
        To fetch a pail of wa... ter
        Jack fell down and broke his... crown
        And Jill came tumbling af... ter.'

ACTIVITY SIX

Playing Names

Once the child can easily sustain drum beating and enjoys playing to your singing, you can begin to get her to imitate rhythmic patterns on the drum. This will help the child to distinguish the different sorts of rhythm in speech. Start by using the rhythm pattern of her name.

As usual, position yourself opposite the child.

Get her attention and tell her to 'Listen'.

Say and beat the rhythm of her name, slowly and clearly, but not so slowly that it loses the sound of the name.

                ! !   ! !
e.g.   Jen-ny or Je/mi-ma

Repeat

Offer the drum to the child.

Even if she can't say her name she may, by now, be able to imitate the rhythmic drum sound of her name.

If she uses the drum to start beating repeatedly, stop her by removing the drum.

You may need to repeat the pattern again and again, but always leave time and space for the child to attempt the imitation each time you play it. Somehow you have got to make it clear that this is a new game.

If she still persists in free beating, try to remove the drum after the correct number of beats. This way you will be showing her, through the sound she is producing, that you want her to play a short pattern.

When the child achieves her drum name, DON'T try to get her to *say* her name as well.

Praise her and repeat the game.

When you feel that she is secure in what she is doing introduce another name with the same rhythmic pattern

!   !

e.g. Da-ddy.

Later on, you can move on to another pattern altogether, but don't rush. The important thing to remember is that music should be fun. If the child senses you pushing her on too quickly she may become resistant.

ACTIVITY SEVEN

Using the Chime Bars

Playing the chime bar demands more control from the child, so don't start using them until she has gained some control on the hand drum. However, if you are having difficulty in getting her to hold a beater, the chime bar may interest her in using it more than the drum. At whatever stage you introduce the chime bars, you should always aim to produce a good clear sound which the child can enjoy listening to. There is not much point in using the chimes as you would a drum and beating in time with them. It is much more effective to use them 'melodically' rather than 'rhythmically'.

VERY EASY

Single Sounds

Place a beater next to the child and ask her to pick it up.

Even if you don't think she will respond to this command, eventually she may, as she learns that to play the chime bar you *need* a beater.

As an introduction to the chime bar sound spend some time playing alternate individual notes, slowly and clearly. First you, then the child, you, then the child, and so on.

Then use the other chime bar and explore its sound in the same way.

As the child gets better at playing accurately, move the bars further away, so that she has to stretch out to find them.

You can use this play to emphasise the careful use of the beaters.

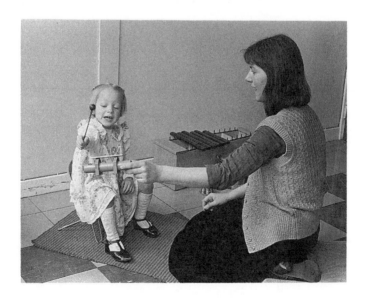

MORE DIFFICULT

Two Note Playing with Colours

When you get the chime bars try to buy different coloured ones as this will help the child to identify the difference in sound, and the difference in sound will in turn help to identify the difference in colour.

A very simple game can be played with your two chime bars.

One is 'High' and the other is 'Low'. (Make sure you can hear the difference!)

Ask the child to pick up the beater you have placed at her side.

Hold one bar in each hand and move them in rotation.

Sing: !   !

    'The high one and the low one,
    The high one and the low one,   Slowly
    The high one and the low one,
    David can play'.

Make up your own simple tune and substitute the correct name.

Try putting the bars high up and then low down
as you sing 'High' and 'Low'.

Play the game again this time singing:

!   !

' The red one and the blue one,
    It's the red one and the blue one,   Slowly
    The red one and the blue one,
    David can play'.

Make sure the child plays the appropriate colour
as you sing it.

Playing chime bars with songs or other instruments

You can use the chime bars while singing songs, but use them sparingly.

Offer one to the child to emphasise the end of a phrase rather than as a continuous background to the singing. This way the child is more likely to make her own vocal sounds as she anticipates the shape of the phrases.

!

e.g. 'BaBa Black sheep, have you any wool?

!

Yes Sir, Yes Sir, three bags full.

!

One for the Master and one for the Dame...'
and so forth

You can combine the chime bars with other instruments to form a small group of sounds.

For example, make sound patterns for the child to imitate, using chime bars, bongo drums and a tambour:

- Two beats on the bongos, followed by one beat on a chime bar

- One beat on the high chime bar, followed by one beat on the tambour and finished by one beat on the low chime bar

Play the patterns slowly and clearly, and look out for any attempts the child may make to give you patterns to imitate. Remember, you are always aiming at 'conversations'.

Activity Eight

Using Rattles

There are many different types of rattles available. You will need to think carefully about your child's ability to hold and use the object when choosing an appropriate rattle. There are some very good African rattles on the market which are available from shops that specialise in ethnic goods.

The first one shown is a long string rattle made of large beans. This type of rattle can be used to swing to and fro between you and the child, to shake up and down or explore in detail. As you can see, Jemima is working hard at catching and shaking as I sing to her in time with the swinging instrument.

The more usual type of rattle is also shown – a small hand-held instrument. Let the child explore the rattle first and then help her to use it rhythmically. You can also use it on the drum head to get a louder sound. It is important to use these instruments sparingly. Otherwise, the listening experience is dulled and the sound becomes too familiar to be of much interest to the child.

Rattle sounds go nicely with drum sounds, so play freely and try to improvise a song as you go, then exchange instruments.

ACTIVITY NINE

Clapping Music

It seems obvious to mention clapping as a musical activity, but it is something which can be overlooked, because it is so simple. For some children clapping to music is one of the few organised activities they find stimulating and it is very helpful to go back yourself to that most simple of musical activities and join with the child in clapping to a song.

You can see that Kelly's interest is held and sustained by our clapping game. We have extended our claps to become exaggerated movements which she finds funny and exciting.

Explore your child's interest in clapping and touching in time. The most important thing to remember in this game is that the shared play you are both engaged in can be extended by either of you, so watch carefully what the child does.

Imitate her as she imitates you, and enjoy the play as she enjoys it. Use simple songs that she knows, or make up your own clapping song:

e.g.   'Clapping, clapping, clapping, clapping,
         Clapping to the Mu-sic.
         Kelly's clapping, clapping, clapping,
         Clapping to the Mu-sic.'

ACTIVITY TEN

Using Chinese Hand Cymbals

Inexpensive, and attractive to the child, these hand cymbals can be used with children with severe disabilities. If the child cannot hold them individually you can suspend them so that the child can feel them and brush them together to make a sound.

Here, Kelly has explored the cymbals, turned them around and succeeded in using them on her own. I am playing a drum in time with her playing as I sing a simple tune to support and encourage her music.

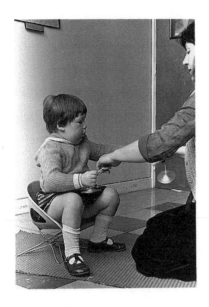

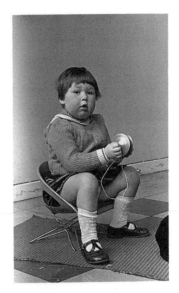

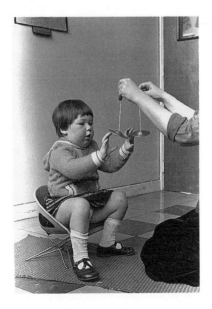

ACTIVITY ELEVEN

Using Horns

The reed horns you can see in the photograph (see p.73) are very good for encouraging closure of the lips and for making the child generally more aware of changes in mouth position. This in turn can help her towards forming mouth positions for words. Blowing is also an important experience in learning to make words.

Getting to know the Horn

Position yourself comfortably opposite the child.

Pick up the horn and blow it slowly and clearly.

Offer the horn to the child.

Let her explore it and then help her to hold it appropriately.

The child may not want to put the horn in her mouth, so let her hold it whilst you blow it again.

It may take some time before the child will try to blow, so don't force her to put it in her mouth.

Even if she can't make a sound, praise her for her attempts and repeat the horn sound yourself.

Offer her the horn again.

EASY

Horn Song

Choose a song you both know and substitute the word at the end of each line with a horn tone.

Keep hold of the horn and offer it to the child at the right moment.

Let her blow it and then remove it as you sing the beginning of the next line.

Although she may not be able to sing the words of the song, the child will be directly concentrating on the phrase length and the position of the word in the phrase:

e.g.   'Polly put the kettle–*horn tone*!
        Polly put the kettle–*horn tone*!
        Polly put the kettle–*horn tone*!
        We'll all have–*horn tone*!' and so forth...

As she gets to know this game, work towards getting the child to keep hold of the horn so that eventually she controls the horn tones herself.

ACTIVITY TWELVE

Using the Xylophone

The wooden xylophone shown here is an ideal instrument for concentrated playing. It offers loads of opportunity for imitation and control – control both of movements and of behaviour. It is, however, the most expensive of the instruments I have discussed. I include it here because you may have the opportunity of influencing a playgroup budget, or of buying one together with some other people.

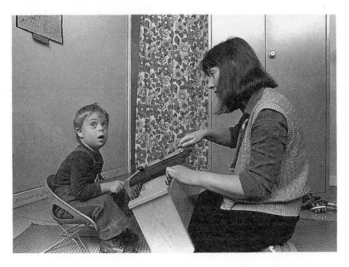

Suggestions for Your Own Playing

You don't need to use all the notes at once. In fact, the good thing about the xylophone is that you can choose a 'scale'. Try putting these different series of notes on the frame:

CDEGACDEGA   EF#ACEF#ACD

CDEFGABC   ABDEGADE

DEFGADEFGA   GACEFF#GA

CDF#GCDF#G   B♭CDEF#B♭CDEF

The xylophone can be used very freely once you have gained some confidence in your own ideas.

You may need to practice counting in time by clapping or using a hand drum.

Then move onto the xylophone, playing up and down the scale you have chosen. Don't try to make complicated tunes, just play each note evenly up and down the scale in time to your counting. Once you can do this, you can begin to be a bit more adventurous by leaping notes and making melodies.

Practice playing to the following counts. (The stress marks above the numbers indicate that you should emphasise the note).

123 123 123 123

123456 123456 123456

12312 12312 12312

1234 1234 1234 1234 1234

12345678 12345678

12 12 12 12 12

Xylophone Games

As you can see from the picture opposite, you can hold the xylophone on your lap so that it tilts towards the child. This reduces the possibility of the pieces springing off. Make sure also that the pieces are pegged from your side of the frame.

Don't worry about playing songs or tunes that you know on the xylophone. You can use it much more freely by making up your own sung melodies over the top of the scale you are using. Practice singing to your own playing.

It will be too much to expect the child to learn to play her own favourite tune on the instrument. What you are aiming for is imitation of WAYS of playing, rather than learning tunes.

EASY

Up and down playing (hard rubber beaters)

This game is really the same as the up and down drum game, although it demands more concentration from the child.

Position yourself comfortably opposite one another.

Get the child's attention by saying, 'Watch!'

Make a very large movement upwards with your arm.

Hold it for a moment and bring your beater down onto one of the tones.

Tell the child it is her turn.

Help her, if necessary, to make her own tone, anywhere on the xylophone.

Repeat, until a nice flow of tones is being played; first you, then the child, and so on.

As you can see, the child will be watching what you are doing and listening carefully to what is happening.

EASY

Glissando game

In contrast to the careful up and down movements you have been making, now show the child a very clear run across the tones, producing a harp-like sound. Start from the child's easiest position, so that if she is right-handed start from your left and draw the beater all the way across the tones in one movement.

Repeat and then let her try to imitate how you have played.

Play alternate glissandi, first you, then the child, until you are playing in time with one another. Then improvise a simple melodic line with your voice. You don't have to use words, just 'La La' softly with the sounds you are making, in time with your movements. You may be surprised to hear her join in with the singing.

Contrasting playing

After the child has learned these two different ways of playing, play together but keep changing your playing from glissandi to up and down tones. Give the child enough time at each sound to feel confident before you change it. Get the child to imitate your changes in playing and then see if you can imitate her changes in playing by letting her play how she likes.

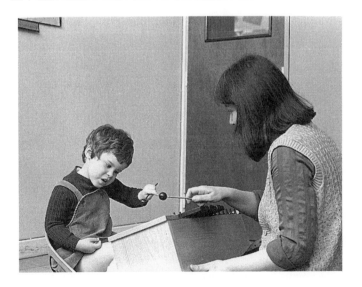

MORE DIFFICULT

Divide the Xylophone

When the child has gained some control at playing, divide the tones so that you have two, and the
child has five or six. You are aiming to increase her
control by limiting where she can play on the
frame.

Leave a gap between your notes and hers, so that
yours are at one end and hers are at the other.

Tell her that she must only play her tones and must
not play yours.

Play your tones together and then switch around
so that the child has only two tones to concentrate
on. Occasionally you must cheat and play her
tones instead of your own, then it will be more
exciting and she will start to cheat as well. This
will demand a lot of concentration, as good games
always do.

Activity Thirteen

Walking to Music

As I discussed earlier, music invites movement, and for those children who are still unsteady walkers, or who need to be helped to balance, music will help them to organise their movements more accurately. The main thing to remember about walking to music is that the music must be at the child's pace. It is no good putting on a tape and expecting the child to be able to move in time.

Unless you are sure that a certain piece of music goes at the speed of the child, use your own singing and drumming. You are infinitely more flexible than recorded music and you can stop and start with the child or slow down, if necessary. Here Claire and I are walking carefully together, and I am singing a walking song as we go. Later on she moves on her own to the music.

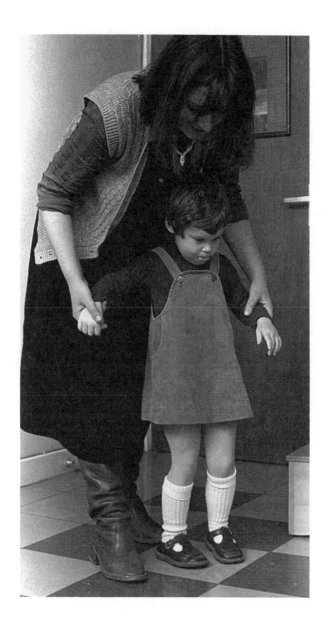

Conclusion

A lot of children have already enjoyed making music and have found it helpful. Playing music with your own child can be a useful way of 'doing something' for her or with her.

Remember, the activities described in this booklet can be used freely so you can adapt them to suit your child. Remember also that YOU are MUSICAL. Try to experiment with your own singing and playing. You will find it becomes easier and easier as you gain confidence. I hope you find this book helpful and that you enjoy making music with your child. Have fun!

The Author

Elaine Streeter trained as a music therapist in 1974 with Paul Nordoff and Clive Robbins. She went on to train as a teacher in special education and was then appointed by the ILEA to work as a music therapist and special educator with young children at the Child Development Centre Charing Cross Hospital. In 1977 she completed a post-graduate music degree at the University of York with the first university-based research dissertation on music therapy in the UK. In 1981 she was appointed Senior Lecturer in Music Therapy at the Roehampton Institute of Higher Education with the brief to develop a new post-graduate training course for music therapists. In 1989 she completed a three-year training course in psychodynamic counselling at the Westminster Pastoral Foundation.

She now works as a music therapist with adults, music therapists in training, and children. She is an approved supervisor for the Association of Professional Music Therapists.

Index

Easy for the Child, More Difficult for You

More Difficult